The New Novello Choral Edition

JOSEPH HAYDN

Mass 'In time of war'
Missa in Tempore Belli
(Hob. XXII/9)

for SATB soloists, choir and orchestra

Vocal score

Revised with a new piano accompaniment by Michael Pilkington

Order No: NOV 072514

NOVELLO PUBLISHING LIMITED

It is requested that on all concert notices and programmes acknowledgement is made to 'The New Novello Choral Edition'.

Es wird gebeten, auf sämtlichen Konzertankündigungen und Programmen 'The New Novello Choral Edition' als Quelle zu erwähnen.

Il est exigé que toutes notices et programmes de concerts, comportent des remerciements à 'The New Novello Choral Edition'.

Orchestral material is available on hire from the Publisher.

Orchestermaterial ist beim Verlag erhältlich.

Les partitions d'orchestre sont en location disponibles chez l'editeur.

Permission to reproduce the Preface of this Edition must be obtained from the Publisher.

Die Erlaubnis, das Vorwort dieser Ausgabe oder Teile desselben zu reproduzieren, muß beim Verlag eingeholt werden.

Le droit de reproduction de ce document à partir de la préface doit être obtenu de l'éditeur.

© 2004 Novello & Company Limited

Published in Great Britain by Novello Publishing Limited
Head office: 14/15 Berners Street, London W1T 3LJ

Preface

The mass 'In Time of War' was composed in 1796 at the height of Austria's long conflict with Napoleonic France. The first performance probably took place on 13 September 1796 in Eisenstadt. It is one of the six masses that Haydn composed for the name day of the Princess Josepha Maria, wife of his employer Prince Paul Anton Esterházy.

For the first performance at Eisenstadt, there was no flute part and clarinets and horns were only used in the 'Qui tollis' and 'Et incarnatus' movements. For a later performance in Vienna, the flute was added for the 'Qui tollis' and the clarinets and horns used throughout the work.

Notes:

Kyrie bar 41. The crotchet given in the sources for the tenor solo is an indication of the fact that the soloists were taken from the chorus. At this point the tenor part has a rest on the second beat, whereas in all parallel situations the tenor part continues immediately.

Credo bar 147. Here, Haydn omits a line of the text: 'Qui cum Patre et Filio simul adoratur et conglorificatur'.

Michael Pilkington
Old Coulsdon, 2004

MASS 'IN TIME OF WAR'

Missa in Tempore Belli

JOSEPH HAYDN

KYRIE

Allegro moderato

* Tenor note 1: ♩ in sources

14

GLORIA

15

18

21

* tenor note 2: d' in sources

32

* see Preface

CREDO

42

* see Preface

48

52

SANCTUS

BENEDICTUS

72

AGNUS DEI